PAGANS
CONQUISTADORES
HEROES
and
MARTYRS

PAGANS
CONQUISTADORES
HEROES
and
MARTYRS

By MERLE ARMITAGE
ASSISTED BY PETER RIBERA ORTEGA

ACADEMY GUILD PRESS

TABLE OF CONTENTS

PRELUDE

by Margaret Phillips

A brief introduction before the reader begins this adventure.

Mr. Armitage with sparkling clarity coupled with a simplicity and ease of style, has unbelievably condensed 500 years of factual, turbulent and complex history into a compact and beautifully written saga as gripping to read as a good mystery.

Most people when thinking of the southwest have the mistaken impression of a forbidding desert over which the streamliners pass swiftly to California. Or, a vast, barren panorama seen thousands of feet below a plane. The land IS vast, stark, barren. The Mojave desert IS desolate, voiceless. But few people know this is one of the most strangely beautiful, unexpected and varied areas on this earth. One of the most rewarding. One of the most fascinating.

The southwest begins with the first glimpse of buttes in West Texas and extends across New Mexico and Arizona, and on into the lonely deserts of Southern California. Just about a thousand miles from east to west and four hundred miles from north to south.

People who have visited this immense land have come away enchanted and awed by the darkly brooding Jemez mountains, the spirit-haunted Sangre de Cristo range, the staggering distances which delude the eye. Awed by the incredible bigness and majesty of nature unencumbered by steel and concrete. Awed ... but with little idea of its variety or its romantic past.

Compared with almost any other portion of these United States, the southwest glows with color, mystery and adventure. The land of Coronado, de Vargas, de Vaca, Alvarado, Oñate, Fray Marcos and the heroic Father Serra. As Mr. Armitage so powerfully portrays, legends rise like mirages from this kaleidoscopic scene. We are reminded of the seven cities of Cibola, Billy the Kid, Kit Carson and Pancho Villa. Further back in the pages of history we encounter the basket weavers, the unknown inhabitants of Mesa Verde, the timeless home of the Navajo, Apache, Hopi, Zuni and many other pueblo populations.

The Spanish came with Coronado and other conquerers upon the indigenous Indian cultures, imposing their way of life, to be followed by the Anglo Saxons. The Spanish came seeking gold. Legend pictured gleaming cities whose jewels would provide wealth for the old world. As they pushed deeper and deeper into the trackless wilderness, they unconsciously discovered a land whose riches today are many times greater than all of Spain.

Providing more recent color are the facts and legends of the Santa Fe Trail, the covered wagon, the Indian trader, the scout, the cowboy, the guide and soldier. All this weaves into the exotic fabric of the southwest.

This has all become a part of our country. What was the motivation that brought the Spanish here? Merle Armitage has with great skill organized this extraordinary tale. It begins, of course, when Isabella of Spain financed that strange, courageous voyage into the New World. Never has there been a more compelling story. One which exceeds with its truth any possible fiction. For this is indeed a book of historical fact. Merle Armitage not only researched history, but made innumerable trips over much of the country he so vividly describes. Here, in but few pages we can follow with ever growing excitement the Conquistadores explorations into vast, unknown America.

Uninformed, we of today had looked upon the southwest as of little importance in the history of the United States. We now stand a little taller and look with new respect tinged with pride, upon a culture rich in faith and courage. We close the book with a new awareness, wanting to comprehend the heart of this land; to know more about its distinctive, ancient civilization.

Surprising is the fact that although cattle and horses are a trademark of this region, not a horse nor a cow was known here before the advent of Coronado!

Such fragments of information are incidental to the wonders awaiting the reader on almost every page, an avouchment of how Christianity came to America, a miraculous page in world history. It provides a new appreciation of the momentous contribution which the Spanish made to our country. These Catholics, for instance, had established a church and school in what is now southeast New Mexico, 22 years before the Pilgrims landed on Plymouth Rock!

This is a book for those who are interested in the how and why of the southwest, seeking an understanding of its culture. If you are an European it will amaze you. If you are an American it will surprise you and make you proud.

FOREWORD

Forewords are strange beasts of literary burden. Supposedly intended to whet the appetite and encourage exploration beyond the title page, forewords are best left unread, or at least abandoned for some idle moment after the book itself has been thoroughly digested.

What, after all, does the average foreword reader demand? He has already bought the book. Even such a minor financial outlay impells the spending of some time in perusing the work, with or without the enthusiastic invitation of a friendly foreword. Surely the solution must lie in a word, here, of appreciation for the author; a brief note on the qualities, personal and otherwise, which make his book particularly endearing.

With this book, however, more than an appreciation, there must come a warning. There are some, those who have felt the energetic impact of the Armitage personality, who will be positively unsettled as they turn the very first page of this small volume. This in itself is no rarity in Armitage productions; he has consistently upset complacency wherever his roving genius has encountered it: In art, in music, in design, even in cooking. But in this book a new and striking image of the man who is Armitage emerges, a beautiful and we pray lasting image of a man captivated by the immensity of a Divine ideal.

There is, in places, high and low, a concept of Merle Armitage as the daring innovator, the adventuresome forerunner of modernity.

The novelty of a deeper Armitage, for those who know and love him, will be welcomed, greeted in fact with optimistic hopes for future works displaying the same spiritual insight into human values.

Someone once remarked about Merle Armitage that the essential quality of his personality is an intuitive grasp of the fitness of things, an urge to organize all materials, no matter the kind, into an ordered design, a natural harmony. Readers of this truly excellent work will not long be left in doubt that this is so; they will soon know the full sweeping force of this passion for design in the pages that follow. Through the dramatic pattern of early Spanish colonial history in the United States, Armitage has threaded the deceptively simple theme of an ardent humanity in touch with Divine Love.

Although the eminently capable assistance of a noted research scholar, Peter Ribera Ortega, has given the cast of historical authenticity of these pages, this book is not a complete analysis of colonial history in the Southwest, nor does it pretend to be. Rather is it a perceptive view of significant phases in that history, so impressive and yet so little understood. Boldly, with imagination, the author tells us something he himself apparently has learned with violence: A great Cause that is loved entails suffering, for there is no love without suffering. And a great Cause that is not loved nor suffered for, is sterile, leaving no trace upon the human spirit. Only love brings to full fruition; only Divine Love lives eternally.

It was this Divine Love that marked pagans and conquistadores alike, and made the heroes and martyrs whose saga Armitage chronicles in this book.

Rev. Francis Tournier, S.T.L.
Editor; New Mexico Register
Santa Fe, February 1960

PREFACE

In the past fifty years, a new understanding of the constructive impact of Spain on the New World has come into focus. Before that time the "black legend" of Spain had sadly misstated the truth of history. A lamentable misunderstanding of the role of Spain and the Catholic Church in the colonizing of the United States was practically universal. The historians and others bred in the biased traditions of sixteenth-century England succeeded in warping the whole picture to generations of Americans. The accomplishments of Spain in their jealous eyes were evil, insignificant and as a final denouement, Catholic! Even such a pioneer historian of integrity as Adolph Bandelier, in attempting to correctly state the case for Spain, was denounced. There are books yet to be written on how the Whigs' misrepresentation of the part played by Spain intrigued, indeed captured, American historians. The grip was only broken a generation or more ago by the enlightened impersonal investigations and writings of Herbert Eugene Bolton. Bolton not only examined the archives on both sides of the Atlantic, but many times he took to the field, with scholar associates, to trace on horseback the journeys of the conquistadores and the padres, and to check thereby the facts. The documentation he thus presented has enabled laymen and historians alike to properly assess our own past. As the scales come into balance, the immense part played by the Spanish becomes poignantly apparent.

The matter of the earliest history of European conquest in America was further clouded by the fact it has been a fixed practice to regard ecclesiastical history, and secular history as two separate and self contained subjects. No modern historian can accept such a premise, particularly in the case of the Spanish, where, at that period in history, State and Church were united as never before or since.

This work is certainly not a history, nor does it have pretensions to even superficially cover the events that took place since Columbus sailed west from Spain. It does aim to pinpoint some of the strange and often unexplained events and movements which succeeded, in spite of every conceivable obstacle, in bringing the image and the meaning of Christ to the New World. It narrows its focus on the American Southwest and does not include the immense energy, faith and accomplishment of the padres who established **El Camino Real** and built a magnificent series of Missions from Mexico to San Francisco. It says nothing of the exploits of Cabrillo, or Vizcaíno or Gálvez, not to mention the saintly heroism of Fray Junípero Serra who accomplished the peaceful occupation of California in 1769.

This relatively small project is concerned with the cement holding together the bricks and stones of history, which can only be of supernatural origin. Even the rugged padres without this grace, never could have withstood the dangers and trials to soul, spirit and body that were necessary to the conquest of so vast a land.

True, there were mistakes, errors and heartbreaking misunderstandings. The Indian revolt in the late seventeenth century was an inescapable and bloody result of a long accumulation of abuse, friction and brutality on the part of Spanish troops. Indian pride was heavily involved.

For years the situation had been in a state of flux. Coronado, with the best of intentions, could not control the men under his command at all times, or in detail. The common soldier is notorious in his vandalism, and the Indian presented a target that released his frustrations and swelled his ego. Conversely, the non-aboriginal population was a heterogenous mixture of Spanish, creoles, castes and ignorant Mexicans, upon whom the primitive Indian looked with contempt because of their moral looseness and frivolity. It is something of a miracle therefore that the padres had been able to impress the word of God on the red man and hold him in check.

When the outraged Indians, after years of hesitation, finally struck, fiendish planning, robbery and fire destroyed haciendas, **estancias** and churches. Twenty-one missionaries lost their lives as well as over four hundred Spanish men, women and children. It is the blackest page in the southwestern history.

The healing answer to all this was the padres' compassion for the red man. In the ideology of the Spanish missionaries, the Indian was a child of God. It was the conviction of the men of God that the Indian possessed a soul worth saving. And against repeated set-backs and tragedies, the missionaries pushed on and made extraordinary sacrifices, despite fantastic odds, and eventually won their long, tortuous and valiant battle. Viewed in the perspective of time, these men seem superhuman and their achievements give the soundest proof to the rightness of the church's attitude and substantiate the theme of this book. The missionaries were not completely lacking in support, as witness the bull **Sublimis Deus** of Pope Paul III in 1537 in which he declared, "The said Indians and all other people who may later be discovered by Christians, are by no means to be deprived of their liberty or the possession of their property, even though they may be outside of the faith of Jesus Christ."

If history may be read without prejudice, especially the truly **reconstructed** history of our time, the part played by the Spanish in the New World takes on its proper and tremendous dimensions. At a time when the good neighbor policy is in the minds of most Americans, it is with pride that we may look back to our rich heritage of Spanish architecture, art and customs. Our creed, "One people under God" is in harmony with the spirit bequeathed to us by Spain. And in viewing this fascinating spectacle set before us by history, it must be remembered that the Spanish knew nothing of democracy. They behaved, therefore, in accord with the decorum, compassion and understanding bestowed upon them by the Spanish and Church disciplines. And by their achievements, they erected a monument of heroism, valor and faith, that forever will be a component of the American consciousness; a part and parcel of the soil of our country.

Chapter 1
THE UNCONQUERED
LAND 1540

A giant ponderosa, victim of lightning and fire, thrusts its skeleton arms towards the sky. Alone on the precipitous slopes of the Sangre de Cristo range, its sinister aspect is heightened by a golden eagle observing every minute object that stirs below. The desert extending from the cool sanctuary of the mountains, lies beaten by the inexorable hammer of the sun. Distant horizons reflect sullen ranges. In between, the torment of other fiery plains. To a casual observer, a forbidding, empty land.

The vast expanse of mesa, flecked with sagebrush, hides a miniature world. There scamper rabbits, squirrels, chipmunks and mice. High above all this gay innocence the

1

watchful hawks and eagles soar in endless, majestic circles. Wily rattlesnakes, in secluded shade, lay coiled to strike. As night replaces the governing sun, coyotes attack. Owls, the silent ones, suck the blood of rodents. Porcupines with bowless arrows squat frightened, as skunks suffocate their adversaries.

But now at high noon the golden eagle departs his watchtower. On a column of thermal updraft he soars, wings motionless to inspect the immensity of his domain. Unconcerned with the purple canyon of the Rio Grande (a deep sabre wound in the desert) or the mirage creating distances, he wheels, concentrating on the active surface life of the lilliputs. Far to the west the vast eroded structure of the Grand Canyon harbors its mile deep river. An occasional snow encrusted peak rises through the shimmering heat. Here and there a mesa pueblo, its ant-like Indians going about their primitive chores, signal awareness of human consciousness. A primeval southwest prostrates itself to the murderous sun.

Leagues southward in the mazes of parched plains and hellish mountains, the natives discern an exotic column in clouds of dust. Pagan sages, medicine men and chiefs hurry into conclave to evaluate the fantastic apparition.

2

Scouts report men white of skin on horses, resplendent in helmets, armor, sparkling uniforms. Prodigiously armed.

Those savages witnessed one of man's great days in history; a breathless moment preceding four hundred years of drama. Thus began a period of courage, pillage, faith, murder, heroism and martyrdom. Terrifying and triumphant. The year was 1540 on the Spanish calendar, and the expedition of Coronado moved significantly across the wastes seeking the evanescent Seven Cities of Cíbola.

Chapter 2
THE FINAL DECISION
1492

It was late afternoon and the trail was hot and dusty. Christopher Columbus, angry that Isabela and Ferdinand had required six and a half years to finally refuse his magnificent plan, was on his way to Córdova en route to France.

Charles VIII would eagerly grasp the opportunity that Isabela and Ferdinand had let slip through their hands. France then, would be the beneficiary of this unique enterprise of the Indies. New lands, great riches in gold and precious stones, converts to the Roman Catholic faith.

With Columbus, riding a second mule, was the faithful Fray Juan Pérez, whose belief in the great enterprise never wavered. The

4

two travelers carried few but important components. Wrapped in Columbus's spare shirt and stuffed in his saddlebag were two treasures, for him the most significant books in the world. One, the **Imago Mundi,** a parchment volume bound in leather had been written around 1410 by Pierre d'Ailly, Cardinal of Cambrai. A rare and comprehensive world geography. The other, the **Historia Rerum** was by Aenas Sylvus. Based on the transcendent ideas of Claudius Ptolemy, it held more accurate information than the **Imago Mundi,** although Columbus was not altogether pleased with it. Some of the projections ran counter to his own beliefs and prognostications. But its learning was immense and of extreme value to him. These volumes held the best contemporary knowledge of the world. To Columbus they were indispensable.

As the afternoon progressed some of the sting of his great disappointment moderated and Columbus began to analyse and chronicle the events of the years that led to such bitter disillusionment.

Ferdinand habitually looked eastward rather than westward. Columbus and his project had never really caught his imagination. Nor was he sympathetic. Columbus was

forced to admit both the looseness of His Majesty's morals and the corruption of his character. The one sustained interest of the King was diplomacy, practices on the level of stealth, duplicity and legerdemain. He loved, for instance, to deceive the King of France. He took a hand in the intrigue of every state or league. The kingdoms of Catalonia and Valencia, bordering on the Mediterranean engendered maritime traditions and the King was solely interested in trade with eastern Mediterranean states. Tricky, bourgeois, and with a roving eye. Columbus had taken his measure on their first meeting. From the outset, Columbus had decided to expect nothing from the King.

But Isabela la Catolica was a very different person. The Queen and Columbus were devout Catholics. They were both intense, similar in character, and about the same age. When Columbus was first presented to her in early May of 1486, she had listened with interest to his plans for the great enterprise. Mutual respect and comprehension were evident and there was admiration on both sides. Isabela, Columbus reminisced, was not the one who had really failed him. The odds had always been against him in the Castilian Court. Talavera,

powerful in the high circles, opposed him. Scientific men, geographers and scholars held different opinions as to the feasibility of the project. And most damaging of all was Columbus' own estimate of the price to be paid for his achievement. The honors and money he had demanded seemed utterly fantastic. Members of the court either were prejudiced or unable to visualize the enormous advantages to Spain should Columbus succeed.

Three times in the past six years Columbus had made his appeal following exhaustive preparations and maneuvers. Three times he had failed. Fray Juan Pérez, continuously helpful to the cause, rode with him now towards France and a new opportunity. Columbus appreciated his loyalty and integrity. Columbus' thoughts constantly returned to Isabela of Castile as his mule toiled up the trail. He recalled her gracious manners; her tact and dignity. She was strikingly handsome, a type of beauty unusual in Spain, auburn hair, clear complexion, blue eyes. She must have experienced deep disappointment at the sad outcome of a glorious prospect in which she had a mystical belief.

The irony weighed heavily on Columbus' troubled mind. Once he imagined he heard the

sound of a hoof striking rocks far in the distance, but was unable to divorce his thoughts from his reverie. He was therefore totally unprepared for the drama of the next moments. Suddenly emerging from the dust of the trail came three mounted men wearing the regalia of the court. Reigning their panting animals, they saluted Columbus and handed him the orders . . . orders with the aura of destiny. Columbus must return at once. The Queen had completed arrangements to finance his expedition, and to provide him with a proper fleet. This was the incredible message.

This switch from meditation on defeat to the reality of victory after years of frustration taxed Columbus' credibility. Arriving back at Santa Fe de Granada, Castile, he learned the details of events that led to this miracle. The years that Columbus had spent arguing his case with geographers and scholars and preparing his proposal for the King and Queen, had made him many friends and allies. Some were powerful. One such influential person was the keeper of the privy purse, Luis de Santangel, on whom Columbus had made a profound impression. The Columbus project for an expedition to the unknown world to the west had stirred his imagination.

He believed the enterprise could be a service to God, Church and Crown. Learning that Columbus had been defeated and was on his way to France, Santangel sought an audience with the Queen. He expressed his astonishment that a project which promised so much, and risked so little, should be abandoned.

Expressing again his admiration for the Queen, her resolute spirit and faith in matters of consequence he begged with her to assert her influence now. Columbus' fanatical belief in the wisdom and the necessity of the voyage, he explained, would lead eventually to others financing the enterprise. This would surely do great damage to the Crown; be a grave reproach to the King and Queen. In a final eloquent plea, he, Santangel, had offered to finance the fleet and the voyage himself.

Impressed, Isabela promised immediate reconsideration, even venturing the suggestion that she could pledge her jewels, a gesture widely heralded through the kingdom. Santangel promised this would be unnecessary as he renewed his warning that Columbus must be overtaken before is was too late.

One of the greatest mutations in the history of man was thus brought to fulfillment. The means were so simple and direct as to have

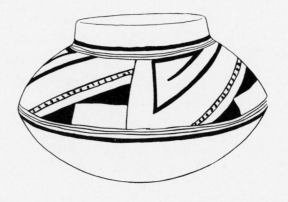

but one explanation. Columbus sailed from Palos on an August morning in 1492. The Niña, Pinta and Santa María were mirrored in the harbor, in a classical Spanish arrangement. As Columbus gave the order and they were bound away, he was filled with an unequivocal conviction that God had moved to bless and mature his plans.

Chapter 3

THE ROOTS OF THE SPANISH CONQUEST 1518

Although Hernando Cortés wrote but five letters commending himself and his exploits, and there exist only a few translations of long lost manuscripts, today we have an impressive literature on the history of men of Spain in the New World. By far the most detailed and explicit account of how the Spaniards maneuvered and fought is the story written by Bernal Díaz del Castillo. At an advanced age, after the chaos of his life as a lieutenant of Cortés' armies, Don Bernal painstakingly wrote down what he had seen and experienced. On these now precious words is based most of the known history of the conquest.

His amazing story has been of immense

help to every historian and scholar and the original manuscript is the most treasured possession of the archives of Guatemala. A copy of it was made and sent to Spain, from which the first published version was prepared by Alonzo Remón, a friar of the Order of Mercy. This version has been translated in many languages. The first English translation was published in London in the year 1800, the work of Maurice Keatinge. In the United States it was published in 1903 and again in 1927.

William H. Prescott's basic material in his **History of the Conquest of Mexico** derives directly from Bernal Díaz del Castillo. The many narratives from Kinahan Cornwallis to Archibald MacLeish's **Conquistador** owe much of their substance to the memoirs of the old soldier who fought with Cortés.

There are as many motives ascribed to the conquistadores as there were men in their armies. Accepting the obvious objectives of conquest: Land, gold, jewels or personal glory, there is one shining thread woven into the fabric which becomes a dominant theme in the pattern. From the lowly privates to the captains-general one element became repugnant to them all. In the hearts and minds of the

handful of Spaniards who accomplished something of a miracle the ruling motivation for victory, once the life of the adversary was known, was to overcome the native's hideous practice of human sacrifice. When its enormity and depravity were understood, the conquest achieved a new goal.

Evil had many dimensions, permeating the air with both a physical and an emotional stench. For Cortés and his men as with the other conquistadores who were to follow, the sinister aspect of the creatures inhabiting the new land became a horrendous menace. Thus the prevention of the obscene ceremonies became a major objective, and all the glittering fascinations of the New World were subjugated into one dominant will; to end the practices so loathsome and unacceptable.

A contemporary Italian painter has suggested the attitude and emotions of the European adventurer in the evil world of Mexico. Giorgio de Chirico wrote: "One of the strangest feelings left to us is the sensation of omen. It will always exist. It is like an eternal proof of the non sequitur of the universe. The first man must have seen omens everywhere; he must have shuddered at each step."

Omens, in the case of the Spanish invaders, became immediate fiendish realities. The sacrificial stones over which victims were bent, as the priests made an incision and removed the living beating heart; the piles of skulls and other human bones, components of every ceremonial courtyard, and the sickening odor of human blood splashed on temple walls, these appalling manifestations hardened the determination of the Spanish to convert the practitioner to a new respect for human life through the example of Christ.

The extent of the faith and the bravery thus engendered can be measured against the "shudder at each step." Thousands of miles from Europe, the Gulf of Mexico separating them from the Cuban coast, outnumbered hundreds of thousands to one, the little band proceeded. Limited in food, stores and the implements of war, they nevertheless went on to conquer a host of repellent savages.

Today, we find great power and immense interest in the art of these primitives, the Pre-Columbians who knew so much about architecture, astrology and art. Theirs was the art of the ceremonies which were a prelude to fantastic sacrifices and death. The strange beauty of Pre-Columbian art is one

of the great finds of contemporary man. It was not created by the Mayan and Aztec and twenty or more civilizations of Mexico as art is created now, but was the handmaiden of ceremonial life, as these rituals were the chief concern of all peoples. The richly carved stones, pottery, jade, and the huge sculpture of these ancient people, seen through our eyes, give but a hint of their sinister aims and purposes.

Looking back on the circumstances of the sudden fall of these savage nations, two things become evident. How was it that they submitted to a mere handful of desperate Spanish soldiers? It then became clear that **Evil** in some of its most subtle forms, had met **Faith** in some of its most unflinching examples.

George C. Vaillant, who was curator of the Mexican Archaeology Museum, and the American Museum of National History, gives us some of the broadest hints and positive explanations. The profound and diligent research in which he reconstructed the whole life of the Aztec civilization produced a multitude of undisputed conclusions which to say the least are sensational.

In the years preceding the Spanish conquest, a sort of mental paralysis prevailed, affecting both high and low. The great and heretofore invulnerable Montezuma, amateur of witchcraft, as well as the chief war lord of the Aztecs, had gone through an appalling experience. This not only severely shook his nerve, but brought on a defeatist attitude completely incompatible with the great man's splendid history and respected position. Nezahualpilli, the chief of Texcoco, had met with Montezuma and they had engaged in an argument; a bitter controversy concerning the soothsayers each employed. Nezahualpilli maintaining after **his** soothsayers in which he had complete confidence, that the land would soon be ruled by strangers. So convinced was he that he made a highly hazardous wager. He offered his kingdom to Montezuma against three turkey cocks, fighting cocks, of course, and the results were to be obtained through a ritualistic game of ball. These stylized ball games were common throughout this area of Mexico; similar to baseball in the United States. Clay figures in complete diaramas that display men on the playing field, the audience in the stadium plus the attendants, have been recently exca-

vated and some are now in American museums and private collections.

In the game which produced such terrifying results, Montezuma took the first two, but Nezahualpilli took the remaining three games. Montezuma was therefore depressed not only because his own soothsayers had been so wrong, but because of the future portents.

Other ominous phenomena came in quick succession. Throughout the following year and every night at midnight a column of fire was seen. A sudden unexplained conflagration destroyed one temple and another was wrecked by lightning, although there was not one cloud in the blue heavens. There appeared a sinister comet which could be seen by day and the usually placid Lake of Texcoco developed sudden and incomprehensible waves of great height and intensity.

Simultaneously with all these terrors, a woman's voice could be heard riding the wind and crying, "My children, we are lost." Monsters began to appear from nowhere and when they were brought before the chief they mysteriously disappeared just as he caught a glimpse of them. The most shattering event was a token in the form of a bird captured by hunters. This bird which was brought before

Montezuma, had a mirror in its head revealing the heavens. But when Montezuma peered within the mirror a second time, it revealed an army of strange men in uniforms and helmets. Montezuma, hardly trusting his own eyes and senses, summoned his soothsayers to explain its sinister meaning. The bird instantly flew away.

One can imagine what effect these ghastly phenomena had on the emotions and the spirit of the people of the Valley of Mexico, and how they were pre-conditioned to defeat previous to the appearance of Cortés and his followers. It was a time of fear, tension, hopelessness and dread, a condition not to be explained by historical facts.

Chapter 4
BISHOP JUAN DE ZUMÁRRAGA

When the Church sent Zumárraga to New Spain a candle of such immense size and special character was lit that its bright beams continue after centuries to light the Americas.

The future Bishop of Mexico was born circa 1476 in the Villa de Durango, señorío de Vizcaya. He was the son of Juan López de Zumárraga and Doña Teresa de Lares a member of the noble Spanish family of Arrazola, Lords of the Tower of Muncharraz. The family was celebrated for its hospitality to the Franciscan friars who passed through Spanish Durango.

Soon after Fray Juan entered the Order of St. Francis his talents were recognized, and

19

a few years after ordination to the priesthood he even attained the important governmental office of Father Provincial, administrator of a Franciscan district. In the year 1527, Charles V spent Holy Week in retreat at the Franciscan convent at Abrojo, where Zumárraga was the Superior. The King ever observant of his subjects, noticed the exemplary spirit of this Franciscan community and the obedience of Zumárraga. The atmosphere was one of tranquillity, zeal for the salvation of souls and genuine Franciscan humility. The Emperor was impressed. On leaving he gave the Superior a large sum of money as alms for the community, despite the diplomatic refusal of Zumárraga. On the Emperor's insistence, Zumárraga, accepted the money and in the spirit of his nature, immediately distributed the entire sum to the poor of the neighborhood, retaining nothing for the Franciscan community.

So enthused was Charles V with Zumárraga that he began to seek a wider use for his talents. Mexico was becoming very important in the affairs of Spain. The Emperor realized the necessity of sending there a prelate who would do justice to the opportunities. So on December 12, 1527 he presented as candidate

for the episcopal seat in Mexico City the humble friar of Abrojo. The truth is that although neither the work nor the dangers of the new world frightened Zumárraga, he humbly feared the dignity of the episcopate. As he refused the offer, the Emperor had to resort to a royal order obliging him to accept the post.

If the Spanish government is to be highly praised for its choice of remarkable ecclesiastical officials in New Spain, the same cannot be said for its selection of civil authorities for the new colonies. Zumárraga was presented with problems of intrigue, deceit and the most incredible civil errors. All this has been recorded and it would be redundant to more than summarize it here. It took a spiritual and mental giant to overcome the handicaps. The first Bishop of Mexico untangled a stubborn web of conflicting purposes, evil and misrepresentation. His victories were many, and it must never be forgotten that it was Zumárraga who introduced and commended Fray Marcos to the Viceroy Mendoza, who, in turn, sent the good padre on his epoch making journey into the Southwest.

Zumárraga, like many sixteenth-century intellectuals, was a segmented thinker, a

Christian humanist who exhibited a great affinity for the ideas of Erasmus. Any fair evaluation, whether merely historical or religious, must place Zumárraga among the five leading figures of that turbulent area. Cortés and Nuño de Guzmán were the military conquerors; Zumárraga and Quiroga were the spiritual conquerors; while the Viceroy Mendoza was the administrative stabilizer of the conquest. And among the five, the star of Zumárraga indubitably shines the brightest. He represented in Mexico the noblest and most enlightened Christian attitude of the time. Some historians and scholars have excoriated Zumárraga for the severity of his punishments, but this is counter to his wide reputation as a humanitarian. And it must be remembered that sixteenth-century Mexico did not belong to the Renaissance but to Dante's world empire. Time and place must ever be considered in arriving at true judgements. There is overwhelming evidence that Zumárraga was one of the strongest Christian links in the chain that stretched from Spain to the conquest of the New World.

In the Mexico of the sixteenth century, the Franciscans were not only intellectuals, but men of action. First, of course, they were

men of God and theologians. In addition they were geographers, explorers, ethnologists, linguists, musicians, sculptors, masters of the liberal arts, architects, farmers, and above all, humanists. Their works were prodigious. They not only built their own monasteries and convents, but they decorated and furnished them. They supervised and directed the work of Indian carvers, carpenters and decorators. To this collaboration of Indian and friar we owe such architectural monuments as the Franciscan convents of Tlaxcala, Calpan, Huejotzingo, Cholula, Cuernavaca, Izamal and other notable structures, which in spite of their abandonment, manifest the high artistic culture of the lesser friars.

Indeed, it has been rightly said that had the Franciscans been allowed more influence in New Spain, the passing from dependence to independence could have been accomplished without war. They understood the Mexican problems; they intermingled with the masses. Their love for the Indians and their educative work gave them authority possessed by no other European, of whatever stature or official position.

Zumárraga was one of the most distinguished, holy and outstanding Franciscans to

trod the soil of North America. It is an ironic twist of history that his great contribution to the culture of Mexico is so little understood, his humanity so relatively overlooked. He pleaded for humane treatment of the natives, deplored the enslavement of the Indians, and actually fought the King's generals in behalf of the natives. To him these savages were intelligent, if primitive, people, and above all, they were human beings. He saw and understood the possibility of saving them for Christ. He perceived that they had many skills, and were learned in astronomy, architecture and mathematics.

As Eduardo Enrique Ríos has written, "Zumárraga is more than a man, he is a genius!" Literally day and night he preached and wrote in favor of the Indians. He was the first to ask mother Spain for a printing press, which finally arrived because of his insistent demands. And from this press came the first book to be printed in the New World. To Zumárraga and the Franciscan family then is due the production of the greatest vehicle for the propagation of faith culture in the New World. Due to them, also, is the formation of the native cults of the sixteenth century. In the famous College of Santa Cruz de Tlaltel-

olco in the city of Mexico, Mexico gained its first great institution of learning, which gates were opened in 1536, a full, significant century before the establishment of Harvard College in New England.

It will surprise many that in these remote days of pioneering the Indians of Mexico were studying Greek and Latin classics. Franciscan masters were busy with research which resulted in such monumental works as the **History of the Things of New Spain,** by Fray Bernardo de Sahagún. Simultaneously friar Andrew of Olmos was instructing Indian doctors in the technique and powers of medicine and other friars were preparing grammars so that the native language might be learned and taught.

Other immense and important projects were in the making. The great architect in Calpan was John of Alameda; and the huge aqueduct of Zempoala was constructed by Francis of Tembleque. The Franciscans built the first hospitals, the first University, operated the first printing press and built the first good roads. And even more, they assembled the wisdom and the myths of the Aztecs.

All this was under the direction of Zumárraga. The role played by the Bishop is im-

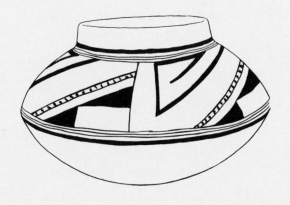

PAGANS

CONQUISTADORES

mense. He was the confidant, friend and supporter of countless discoverers and explorers who brought credit to the civilized world, and converts to Christianity. Among his notable protégés was, of course, Fray Marcos de Niza.

In progressing through subsequent chapters, the reader should keep in mind that Zumárraga was back of many enterprises and bold schemes which were to spread the word of Christ across millions of square miles of New American territory. He was indeed moved by the power of faith. He shared a religious zeal with St. Paul; he possessed the sort of practical cultural outlook which later guided Benjamin Franklin, and the administrative discipline of the modern age.

Chapter 5
DE VACA 1533

The forces which brought Christianity to the New World are mysterious and fascinating. Indomitable men, inscrutable events and sagas of courage and fortitude approaching the miraculous, are encountered without end. None is more improbable than the part played by Alvar Nuñez Cabeza de Vaca and his three companions. De Vaca was a remarkable man of education and breeding. His achievement was to inspire, by indirection, the greatest of the Spanish expeditions.

A greatly simplified version of the steps which led to the exploration of what is now a major area of the United States, would first place the torch in the hands of de Vaca; then in those of the Spanish Viceroy Mendoza who sent the robust Fray Marcos to reconnoiter; and finally to the organization of the army

of exploration headed by Coronado. Any single link in this series of heroic operations was far more audacious than fiction would dare to be. Nor can these extravagant projects be mentioned without crediting the decisive role of the Church. Its devout followers were heroes in the true sense.

Spanish explorers came and roamed over a a region of swamps, sand and luxurious growth; indeed gave it its name, **La Florida** or land of flowers. The whole European continent sent delegations, for, in addition to the Spanish, the French, Dutch, Danish and English had made successful tries to colonize this exotic extension of the North American continent. Ayllon came looking for Utopia. And it was Ponce de León, seeking the **Fountain of Youth** among the Bahamas, who actually discovered the Florida Peninsula.

Then had come Pánfilo de Narvaez. Having lost an eye in a violent incident with Cortés at Vera Cruz, he was to suffer many hardships, with disaster finally ending his swashbuckling career. His booming voice commandered two hundred and fifty men including de Vaca as he marched up the west coast of Florida seeking fabled areas, and particularly a bizarre tribe of natives who were said to

28

wear golden hats. Finding only hostile Indians, he turned at about the point where Tallahassee now stands and proceeded back down the coast. He was forced to kill his horses; while his army lived on the flesh of the animals, they fashioned boats using the horsehide stretched over small timbers. Then began the most ill advised of all of Narvaez' adventures. He and his party set sail for Mexico across the treacherous gulf. His foredoomed expedition ran into heavy storms. Most of his men were drowned in hurricanes, or washed ashore to encounter hungry cannibals. Among those who did survive, four landed on the coast of the present state of Texas and for more than six years three were captives of the Indians, with all the agony this entailed. De Vaca, the fourth man, reached Galveston Island alone, and was held captive until his escape more than a year after his rescue from the sea. Eluding his captors, he fled inland and lived lonely years as a trader. Then he miraculously met three other escapees from the Narvaez adventure and the Indians. The Spaniards were Dorantes, Castillo and Esteban, the latter a Moorish slave who was to have a colorful history in the Southwest.

The four men journeyed west. Their appearance alternately excited worshipful interest or dangerous native hostility. Eventually due to the artifacts the party fashioned, they came to be regarded as workers of miracles and pious men. The holy cross in the hands of de Vaca, and the decorated gourd carried by Esteban the Moor, were accepted as proof of supernatural powers. Indians followed them, seeking cures. These consisted mainly of prayers and making obeisance to the cross. The group became known as **Children of the Sun.** Esteban mastered the native language, and acted as spokesman, elevating their progress to a precarious sort of triumphant march. At times the four men attracted hundreds of followers. They brought the word of God and the faith that restores.

The impression left by these men was profound and permanent. Years later, as Coronado and other Spanish travellers crossed the enormous wastes of the continent, echoes of de Vaca and his party, of their kindness, cures and ministrations, persisted. Four strong men had passed through the wilderness, and their mercy and faith had rippled out in ever widening circles. The works and words enacted and spoken in the

vast solitudes are to this day still reverberating.

After weary months of travel the castaways finally arrived at the Rio Grande, sore of foot, ragged and hungry. They had encountered the great river at a point north of the present El Paso. Here they met natives who lived in permanent abodes or pueblos and raised beans, squash and maize. Resting among friendly Indians and in comparatively comfortable surroundings, they learned of villages further upstream; of natives who fashioned artifacts and wove cotton fabrics; informations of the greatest future consequence.

From this rejuvenating experience, the quartet continued west and south. Through unimagined hardships in the heat of the desert, plagued by thirst and hunger, they emerged at last into the lush Sonora Valley. Here they were told of rich settlements to the north, and for the first time Europeans heard hints of fabulous places later identified as the famed Seven Cities. From this fertile country they were assisted by guides who led the party through a succession of habitations to the Yaqui River.

Here occurred the most sensational and joyful episode of an incredible adventure.

Castillo discovered an Indian wearing what was unmistakably a component of Spanish gear. A necklace from which dangled a small buckle used in a sword belt. Sewed into the buckle was a horseshoe nail! This happy proof that Spanish troops were near was electrical. On close questioning, the Indians revealed that the buckle had been brought by men with beards like their own, whom the Indians innocently claimed had come from heaven.

Three years previously a company led by Diego Guzmán had reached the Yaqui River a short distance downstream. The natives correctly described the men as "on horses, with lances and swords." It was obvious to the four weary men that their worst days were over. As they continued their journey south, they frequently encountered campsites of the Spanish. Some days later, de Vaca came upon four Christians on horseback. It is doubtful which was more surprised. The Spanish, seeing European men in such outlandish attire and in the company of Indians, were speechless. De Vaca recovered first and spoke to the Spaniards who took the quartet to their Commander, Diego de Alcaráz. Listening to their amazing story which he only half believed, he nevertheless decided to conduct

them to Culiacán. Here they were welcomed and further questioned by the delighted Mayor Melchior Díaz.

If the story of the journey of the four men were true, Díaz knew how vastly important it was to the Spanish plans. After a revitalizing rest, he personally escorted them to Compostela. The Governor, Nuño de Guzmán was fascinated by the story. If he was a hard and seasoned fighter he was also a gracious host. He gave them clothing to cover their nakedness and entertained them in the Governor's quarters. This luxury had a curious unreality to these men who had wandered for years in the wilderness. So unaccustomed were they to civilization that de Vaca explained, "for many days I could bear no clothing, nor could I sleep except on the bare floor."

The travellers, suitably clothed and mounted, were soon on their way to Mexico City. Their arrival and tumultuous welcome coincided with the happy celebration of the Vespers of St. James. Both Viceroy Mendoza and the conqueror Cortés extended every courtesy. De Vaca bcame a guest at the Viceroy's Palace. The reports of de Vaca and his companions were naturally of the greatest interest to the Viceroy. For many days the party was

33

HEROES

MARTYRS

interrogated; they had obviously been far beyond the territory surveyed by Guzmán and his forces, and de Vaca brought tales of fertile valleys, food in abundance, handsome blankets, turquoise, emeralds and buffalo robes. Riches! The Viceroy and his staff were particularly interested in the accounts of Indians who had told de Vaca of very large Indian houses. There had been mention of gold, antimony, iron and copper.

This information came at a very opportune time. Could the four refugees have brought news of another Mexico to conquer, or another El Dorado? Possibly they had described the fabulous Seven Cities of Cíbola, which Guzmán had vainly sought. Officialdom, and in fact all of Mexico City, soon tingled with excitement.

For misery, tragedy and pathos, the adventure of de Vaca and his companions is a world classic without parallel. It surpasses Homer's **Odyssey**; the vast difference that separates fable from truth. Yet in this saga of suffering and fortitude the one thing that arrested and held the interest of the public were the tales of cities to the north where the population was rich, and the houses large! This irony

34

served its purpose in the chain reaction of destiny.

The courage to accept one's fate, or in more exact words, the **faith** that generates confidence in the ultimate destiny, gives a man the capacity to survive. Cabeza de Vaca had this faith to a sublime degree; it met the supreme test. It provided him with unlimited courage and remarkable physical stamina. Danger reacted on him as heat treatment on steel . . . it hardened his strength and matured his faith.

This comparatively soft European bred human being, lost in a hideously hostile land of cacti, thirst and thorns, among poisonous snakes and copper-colored savages, with no discernible goal or future, nevertheless survived.

The mysticism of religion, the limitless possibilities of faith, became a living reality he had never suspected. His kind ministrations to others; his own spiritual and physical survival became interlinear with an ageless and universal experience.

Chapter 6

THE CASE OF FRAY MARCOS

Of all the colorful characters encountered in the history of New Spain, one of the most intriguing is Fray Marcos de Niza. Here was a man of God in a heroic mold. Described as a missionary-adventurer, he certainly was much more than that.

Fray Marcos was born in Nice in the Duchy of Savoy. He crossed the Atlantic when this voyage required first rate courage, and became a veteran of the New World when a very young man. At about the time Culiacán was being founded by Guzmán, and while de Vaca was a slave in Texas, Fray Marcos arrived in Santo Domingo as a missionary to that turbulent island. This was in 1531, and shortly

afterwards he departed for Guatemala. Fortunately he arrived in time to go with Alvarado to South America. In Peru he met Pizarro and witnessed the execution of the Inca Atahualpa in that extraordinary country. He was present when Alvarado sold his rights in the conquest of Ecuador to Almagro, and by 1536 he was back in Guatemala.

From there he wrote to Bishop Zumárraga about his revealing experience in Peru, following which the prelate summoned him to Mexico. He arrived in April 1537, and is said to have walked the entire distance barefooted.

The undercurrent of Church resentment against the conquistadores' treatment of the natives is demonstrated by what transpired while Fray Marcos was the house guest of Zumárraga. The Bishop listened to his recital of the shocking cruelties to the Indians; had him put it all in writing, and then brought him and his document to the Viceroy Mendoza. Both men were indignant, and copies of Fray Marcos' statements were sent to Spain where Las Casas used it with telling effects in his then sensational book **Destruction of the Indies.**

This was at the exact moment that Mexico was trembling with excitement over the ad-

ventures of de Vaca and when Mendoza was deliberating the most practical manner in which to confirm the stories and the riches to the north. As Fray Marcos was already a marked man, his selection by the Viceroy for one of the most significant adventures of sixteenth-century North America was natural and highly applauded.

Zumárraga wrote, "This Father is reliable, of approved virtue and of fine religious zeal." Father Ciudad-Rodrigo, the Franciscan Provincial declared that Fray Marcos was "skilled in cosmography and in the arts of the sea, as well as in theology." The Viceroy himself gave eloquent testimony to Fray Marcos and the man to be appointed his companion, Fray Onorato, "these friars have lived in the neighboring countries, they are habituated to hardship, experienced in the affairs of the Indies, conscientious and of exemplary conduct."

But Fray Marcos possessed other qualities which both Zumárraga and Mendoza had recognized. The pious Fray Marcos in addition to remarkable physical stamina, had imagination and an ability to dramatize himself that stamped him as a born missionary. He gave his prodigious optimism to everything he

touched and would have been a distinguished man in any age.

The political-military climate of New Spain was boiling; jealousy and intrigue were rampant. Cortés had been enjoying the fruits of success. Velásquez in Cuba, vexed that Cortés had achieved the great admiration of Charles V in Madrid, had sent Pánfilo de Narvaez and an army to Mexico to arrest Cortés and all his followers. This was on the theory that no one had commissioned Cortés to conquer the Aztecs. For, acting on his own initiative Velásquez maintained that Cortés should be reprimanded and punished. Cortés had thereupon proceeded to absorb Narvaez' army into his own and the intended coup of Velásquez simply resulted in furnishing needed reinforcements for Cortés.

There was considerable confusion as to who was in authority. Months were spent in jockeying for diplomatic advantages. Charles V was the final authority, and as it was likely that the scrambling Soldiers of Fortune might get out of hand, the King appointed a supreme authority for new Spain in the person of Antonio de Mendoza. He assumed the army had completed its mission and it was time for the state to take over.

When Cortés finally released the captive Narvaez he "went bawling back to Cuba." To pacify both Governor Velásquez and the ambitious Narvaez, the always resourceful Charles sent Narvaez on an expedition to Florida. Here he met with disaster, but not before he inadvertantly freed de Vaca to begin the miraculous journey that produced rumors of wealth in the vast territory to the north.

Internal strife was practically without end, it is unnecessary to record more of it here. The Narvaez debacle had, through the de Vaca eight year adventure, given Mendoza encouragement in his desire to gain more substantial proof of the legendary Seven Cities of Cíbola.

What the source of this legend was, none could say. But it was persistent. Born possibly of wishful thinking, it permeated every mind among the conquerors of Mexico . . . particularly the restless young men, ambitious for new worlds, new triumphs. Although the Seven Cities might be beyond the furtherest reaches of the imagination, no one, certainly not the conquerors, wanted to believe it. Cíbola, in contemporary minds, **must** exist.

The man who determined to outsmart his

enemies and be the first to find the Seven Cities was, of course, Cortés. All conquistadores and all potential conquistadores claimed they were not interested while at the same time bending every energy to finance and outfit an expedition. It was an amusing, if brutal competition, and occupied the thoughts, efforts and the full time of every likely candidate.

Following his customary psychology Cortés planned one swift move. He assembled three ships in the Pacific at Acapulco. Intending to lead this expedition himself, Cortés put all his money into it. He would proceed up the coast to the neighborhood of the 34th parallel, and then strike inland to Cíbola. No one at that time was aware that the continent bent sharply to the west, and that any northward journey by sea took the ships further and further away from the fabled cities. This venture was to cost Cortés his fortune, plus the jewels of his wife.

On some pretext Cortés was recalled by the shrewd Mendoza and the expedition was placed in the hands of his Captain, Ulloa. Cortés dispatched Ulloa for Cíbola in July 1539 with supreme confidence. Inasmuch as the expedition sailed under the auspices of

Cortés, it could not fail. Cortés never failed!

Mendoza with great deliberation, had the boastful negro Esteban (who made the journey with de Vaca) brought to audience. It is simple to construct a word picture of what probably happened when the bragging Esteban was brought into the Palace of the Viceroy for questioning.

"Had Esteban," asked the Viceroy, "by some mere chance during his glorious adventures ever heard of a place called—ah—what was its name now?"

"Cíbola!" exploded Esteban.

"Ah, yes, Cíbola" Mendoza purred. "Unusual city, said to be fairly wealthy and lying somewhere in the north?"

"Yes full of gold, I was there," declared Esteban.

"What?" snapped the Viceroy, rising from his great chair.

"No. I mean to say I could **go there.**"

"Ah," smiled the Viceroy. "Suppose you think carefully about it. To yourself. Until tomorrow."

Immediately and quietly Mendoza conferred with Fray Marcos. He and Esteban were to set out to carry the faith to the Indians in the wilderness and **possibly** they might even-

tually come upon the Seven Cities of Cíbola!

Whatever the character of Esteban, he had a reputation for getting along with the Indians, great physical courage, and he knew at least part of the route. A perfect combination. One that could save the government the immense expense of sending a mounted expedition to the wilderness, **before** there was exact knowledge that the fabled cities existed. Prudent, wise and practical! Esteban was to precede Fray Marcos by a week or more.

The account written by Fray Marcos on his return from his northern journey has been the source of much speculation and controversy. The instructions given him by Viceroy Mendoza were necessarily all inclusive, and were written more for the eyes of the King than for Fray Marcos. He travelled among exceedingly friendly and hospitable Indians, most of the way, and certainly amassed a great deal of information of a pertinent nature. As a symbol, it was agreed that things being normal, Esteban would send back a cross the size of a hand. More encouraging findings were to warrant a larger cross, and really significant events or discoveries were to be manifest by a large cross.

It was not too many weeks after Esteban's

departure that Fray Marcos received a cross as tall as himself, with instructions for him to hurry! As Fray Marcos was very experienced with Indians, he was forced to hold his own enthusiasm in check. To hurry might arouse suspicions.

All along the route, Fray Marcos found evidence of great wealth coming from cities to the north. Most of the Indians knew of Cíbola, and many had been there on trading expeditions. Some of them assured the good padre that "they had been there many times." And there were ample evidence of these visits. Buffalo robes, clothing made from wool and jewelry of turquoise; all they claimed had come from Cíbola. It was indeed good news.

Fray Marco planted crosses, took Spanish-style possession of the fairest lands and the best cities as he went. He spread the word of Christ everywhere, and he made friends. The welcome he received was proof of that. But it must be remembered that Esteban the Moor was an ambitious man who loved wealth. There is much evidence to support the fact that he was more than free with the Indian girls along the way.

When Fray Marcos reached a region only a few days march from Cíbola, he was pre-

44

sented with shocking news. Esteban had been murdered, and many of the members of his party, Indians from the south, had likewise met death.

There are many versions of what happened. Some historians believe that warnings of Esteban's conduct with Indian women had reached a Zuni pueblo (Hawikuh, one of the cities of Cíbola) and they were ready for him. But the story told Fray Marcos by the survivors was that Esteban had sent his couriers on ahead to announce his arrival. They had brought back word that the inhabitants were hostile, and warned Esteban not to approach. Esteban in his arrogance did approach, was met by the chiefs. He tendered his decorated gourd as a symbol of omnipotence. Immediately he was repudiated by having his symbol thrown down. He was then put into prison and stripped of all his belongings. Next morning, in attempting to escape, Esteban was shot, several arrows piercing his body. Most of his large party were likewise the victims of the outraged Indians.

Fray Marcos, fearful of what might happen if he ventured too close with other Indians, made one cautious observation of the city of Hawikuh, and departed homeward. "And so

I returned more satiated with fear than with food," the dear Fray Marcos says, "because the Indian men as well as the women, made great lament for the people who were killed at Cíbola."

Fray Marcos' report with complete candor says, **"I do not place here many details because they have nothing to do with the case ... I only tell what I saw and was told me of the countries where I went and of those of which I was given information, for to give it to the Father of our Order, who may advise him, or to the Assembly at whose command I went, that they give it to the Most Illustrious Lord, the Viceroy of New Spain, at whose request they sent me on this journey."**

All the earlier historians, Bandelier, Bancroft, Winship Shea and others, understood Fray Marcos' report, as he went without equipment for recording distances, and did not keep a log or diary. He therefore, as he himself stated, turned in a report that recorded only the essence of his discoveries and his information.

A few modern historians take sharp issue with this report, and some have dissected it under a microscope and found many discrepancies. Some have pointed out various impos-

sibilities and at least one had called the pious Fray Marcos "the lying Monk." Not being a historian I feel these disputed matters can be left to men who are more interested in the fungi on the trees than in the forest.

In the light of modern semantics, the searcher for truth is compelled to ponder deeply one word which is the key to a misunderstanding of the first magnitude. The word is **treasure.** The riches described and constantly mouthed by the Indians were a true evaluation. To these savages, living in a world without water, an environment of bristling and hostile flora and fauna, of jagged, timberless mountains, of almost unendurable heat, the country to the north, with its rivers, its gardens, its sheep, wool, vegetables, grain, textiles and houses, was a land of wealth. These were the only riches the Indians knew, the only wealth that had a meaning for him. Gold, silver or precious jewels would not have been worth his effort to carry or collect. Treasure of this description was as worthless as was uranium only a few years ago.

To the European mind, **wealth, riches, treasures** meant only gold, silver, precious stones and man-made artifacts. Reality to the

Indian proved a natural prevarication to the Spaniard mentality. It is a semantic snare which disillusioned a Coronado, but gave Christianity a new empire, and the world a magnificent and increasingly valuable land.

Those who have condemned Fray Marcos have overlooked a truth that in its very simplicity failed to register with men bent on destroying the reputation of a courageous and pious friar, whose faith unlocked the door to an immense potential. What the critics failed to discern is that Fray Marcos **was** a great man of God, a giant in fortitude, integrity and faith. He did, beyond any dispute, set in motion "the greatest exploring enterprise ever undertaken in the New World."

Following the Coronado expedition, Fray Marcos retired to Jalapa, Mexico, to be with members of his own Order, the Franciscans. Later he died "with a smile on his lips" for he well knew that the Cíbola of **his** dream was the carrying of the faith into the unknown, and this he had accomplished through his optimistic report to Mendoza. The Church had again made good use of military conquest!

Chapter 7
CORONADO MARCHES
1540

The Coronado expedition is one of the best documented and least understood of the great historical explorations. The expectations of its leader or its powerful group of sponsors were never achieved. But it brought to future civilized attention a vast land that in both gold and souls, has yielded a harvest never dreamed of by its most sanguine supporters. As with Columbus, Coronado died without knowing the potential extent of his achievement. But his was a brave band. The distances they covered were immense, their suffering extreme, and their disappointments acute.

Don Francisco Vásquez de Coronado led an expedition which developed many dramatic incidents and elements. In the beginning, at the Compostela rendez-vous and at a time

when the splendor of the encamped forces were at their height, there came strenuous objections to the plan. The newly established provinces of Mexico were being stripped of their best fighting men for the expedition. Was it safe or prudent to leave the newly conquered land with its defenses so weakened and vulnerable?

The long trek to the north and the attitude of its leader has been variously interpreted by historians. It is significant that the best informed men believe that Coronado would have preferred a far more humane treatment of the Indians than was accorded them by his men and officers. The two years and comparative short visits of Coronado's men have left an indelible impression on the Pueblo Indians, and is deeply rooted in their traditions

Members of the Coronado expedition discovered the Grand Canyon of the Colorado, and the supplementary expedition by Alarcón proceeded up the Gulf of California and as far along the Colorado River as the present city of Yuma. In what is today New Mexico, Coronado established his winter quarters. He visited the pueblo of Acoma, the Sky City, and Taos, and his descriptions depicted the pueblos

much as they are today. En route to the mythical riches of Quivira, he crossed the plains of what are now the panhandles of Texas and Oklahoma, and penetrated to the Arkansas River in Kansas. He was intrigued by the roaming bison, understood the possibilities of the plains becoming future cattle ranges. He visualized the potentials of a new empire.

The generations who followed Coronado into this immense and potent country have profited by the riches Coronado missed. They have mined the ore from the mountains, refined the oil from beneath the land where Coronado's men first marched, and in cattle raising alone, have yielded more wealth than was promised by the Seven Cities of Cíbola. As Zumárraga, Mendoza, Fray Marcos and others hoped and believed, Coronado brought to the Christian world a land more prosperous and powerful than all of present day Spain. It therefore must rank as one of history's most romantic and fruitful adventures.

The pre-Coronado situation in New Spain was both a proud and a vexing one for the king. Cortés, victorious in the conquest, was arrogant and clamoring for new adventures. But he was only one ambitious conquistador

among many others who longed for equal fame. Hundreds of young blades had arrived from Spain with extravagant ideas of conquest and riches. They were ready to join any likely adventure in what seemed limitless possibilites.

The King aware of all this, played a trump card. He sent Antonio de Mendoza to New Spain as Viceroy, and Mendoza was a tremendous man. He had the strength and the cunning to check the restless Army, and the skill of a Metternich in using it to advantage. Intrigue was running high and rumors seemed to spread faster than runners could take them. Although Zumárraga and the Church insisted on civilized treatment for the Indians and were intent on saving souls, the exploration was generally welcomed first for its material rewards as well as a means of spreading the faith in Christ.

Cortés had made a trip to Spain, and returned looking for new worlds to conquer. The great unexpected territory to the north held the great fascination. But Cortés was too eager and impulsive for Mendoza. Political and social elements had to be considered. The man selected for such an important command must be a man with a name, and a gentleman.

Coronado seemed to offer every qualification. Educated at the University of Salamanca, he was a Spanish grandee, and recently married the daughter of the Treasurer in Mexico City. And the Treasurer was very well connected indeed!

Mendoza very impressed with Fray Marcos' report, had interpreted the hostility of the Cibolans as that of men defending their riches. When news spread through New Spain that Cíbola had been found, Coronado was almost embarrassed with applications for his expedition. Hundreds of young men rushed to join; it was a duplication of Cortés' conquest of Mexico, possibly even greater.

Guns and powder, arms and armor, doublets and lances, all were polished and in readiness, and hundreds of horses, cattle and supplies were made ready. Castañeda, a member of the expedition who became its historian comments, "When the Viceroy saw what a noble company had come together, and the spirit and good will with which they all presented themselves, knowing the worth of these men, he would have liked very much to make every one of them the Captain of an army."

The Coronado party was one of the proudest that ever set out to conquer new worlds.

The essential values of seeking gold and conquest, and the Machiavellian machinations which had enabled it to march, produced an intoxication that affected every one from Captain to Indian herders. As they passed in review there at Compostela, both Viceroy Mendoza and Coronado inspected them, a brilliantly shining army of eleven hundred soldiers, plus hundreds of animals.

A striking feature was the mixture of odd pieces of European armor with a prevalence of native arms. The muster roll notes that the horsemen took their own lances and swords as well as other weapons, in addition to the arms declared. Included in the total ensemble were bows and arrows, clubs, spears, javelins and other primitive weapons which had been used by the Aztecs and Tarascans during the Spanish conquest.

If to our modern values the target expectations seem empty, it must be remembered that the Church supplied an overtone of piety which to some degree affected every Spanish soul. Erna Fergusson in her foreword to **The Adventure of Don Francisco Vásquez de Coronado** says, "We think of the conquistador as seeking gold, as men of all ages have done. But he was inspired too, by a desire to extend

the blessing of Christianity to the uttermost ends of the earth. This missionary motive had much to do with his invincibility, and with his high personal courage. Times are different, but brave men are the same in all times; and none were ever braver than the band Coronado led from Compostela in tropical Mexico to the prairies of Kansas."

If any man in the expedition doubted its spiritual aims, there was the constant reminder in the person of the friars. Armed only with the cross, they walked beside the mounted nobles, withstood the common sufferings and gave aid to the army and the native personnel alike. In one of the early reports of preparations for the **entrada**, Bishop Zumárraga wrote, "The Viceroy wishes to send friars ahead without arms, that the conquest may be Christian and apostolic, and not a butchery." Following the return of Fray Marcos on his first trip of reconnaissance, Mendoza wrote, "In our day God our Lord has been pleased to reveal vast lands wherein his Holy Name may be known and adored, and his Holy Faith and the Catholic Church extended."

This is a side of the conquistadores that has been little stressed. Actually, Fray Marcos

joined the Coronado expedition not only as a guide who had been over a portion of the route, but as the spiritual head of the expedition, and the leader of a group of apostles en route to a new missionary frontier.

What the American Southwest gained by the Coronado expedition cannot be overestimated. The first cattle and the first horses were brought by these soldiers to a land that now regards cattle and horses as its trademark. Coronado, of course, suffered intense disappointment for his was the immediate point of view. Every foot of the way brought new discouragements, as the **arid zona** looked more barren and forbidding with every forward league. Future travellers gave Coronado's description their approval, and contracted it into Arizona.

But the bitterest disappointment came when the army reached Cíbola or Háwikuh. Not gold and wonderous multi-storied stone houses encrusted with precious jewels, but the mud pueblos of the Zuni, the Indians who had killed Esteban the Moor and defeated his followers.

Adding further pain to this sickening discovery, Coronado himself was wounded. Not in glorious battle leading his valiant troops

against the savages, but in the embarrassing predicament of falling off his horse. In the confines of the Cíbola which he had taken without resistance, he was forced to spend a month in bed! If Cortes ever heard the news it must have merited a sardonic smile.

While the Spaniards encamped at Cíbola, known to us as the Zuni pueblo in New Mexico, Coronado dispatched his next-in-command, Pedro de Tovar on a trip of investigation, hoping to find the rich and "real" Cíbola. During this investigation Tovar ventured as far as the present pueblos of Oraibi and Walpi, finding the Indians there cautious but friendly. Here they obtained information about a large river, and were told that deep in its canyon was the orifice from which "man entered upon the earth."

When Tovar returned, Coronado sent Don García López de Cárdenas with twelve men to investigate the river. They journeyed via Oraibi where they obtained guides. This band of Spaniards without doubt were the first Europeans to look upon the Grand Canyon and the great Colorado River. The spot at which they viewed this awesome sight must have been somewhere near the present Desert View. The impact of the Grand Can-

yon and the river below at this point is absolutely stunning.

The Coronado expedition from then on became a series of frustrations, anxieties, suffering from winter weather, fights with the Indians engendered by the Spanish arrogance and cruelty, revolt and inability to find gold or treasure. Except for side trips to such regions as the Grand Canyon, the present Taos, Ft. Sumner, and exploring southward down the Rio Grande, the Coronado trail is well defined. From Culiacán it has proceeded northward through Los Corazones, to a point somewhat west of the present Tombstone, thence northeast, via various settlements to Háwikuh (Zuni) then east to Acoma, perched on a high mesa. From there the armies proceeded to Tiguex, as this is the name the Spaniards gave to the region that extends from Isleta and Albuquerque to above Bernalillo. They wintered in this locale. The Indians in almost all cases were friendly with the newcomers, but time and the actions of the soldiers seems to have made them eventually hostile in every case. Revolt inevitably followed.

During the stay in Tiguex, the maddest of all the mad Coronado fantasies was realized.

An Indian with a wild imagination and a very convincing eloquence, persuaded Coronado and his followers that the real riches of the vast domain lay to the east and north . . . a mythical land known as Quivira. This Indian nickamed the Turk, explained that in Quivira there was a river three miles wide, fish as big a horses, etc. . . . There was, he said, a heavy traffic on the river, great canoes manned by twenty men paddling, ten on each side. The owners sat under awnings at the end of each boat, and the canoes used sails to help them up the river. Almost everyone in this country, explained the Turk, used plates of silver and drank from jugs and bowls of solid gold. Coronado immediately planned to march. To the frustrated conquistador this was an easy tale to believe, but it proved the greatest hoax of the entire exploration.

When Coronado had passed what is now Dodge City, he followed the Arkansas River northeastward to Great Bend, then east crossing many tributaries. It was summer, the country was green and beautiful. But where were the houses and the wealth? The settlements consisted of round lodges, probably thatched with grass, and the tepee, with smoke emitting from the top of each. These primitive

dwellings housed the nearly naked Wichita Indians. During a stay of possibly four weeks in Quivira, Coronado either saw or was informed of at least twenty-five settlements. But the gold proved to be the roaming buffalo, the verdent grass, and the clear flowing streams. It is significant that Udden the archeologist, prior to 1890, unearthed in this area bits and fragments of late fifteenth century chain mail armor. Other fragments were found by Wedel in a cache pit and refuse heap, on the little Arkansas River. The metal rings of the armor averaged about an inch in diameter. Obviously these were left by Coronado's disappointed men.

The return of the Coronado party from Quivira to Tiguex, the winter spent there, the serious injury of Coronado, and other vicissitudes and adventures, makes another historical chapter and is most sympathetically covered by Bolton in his superb **Coronado: Knight of the Pueblos and Plains.** Many other historians have dealt with the whole Coronado expedition in a satisfactory fashion including George P. Hammond in his **The Adventure of Don Francisco Vasquez de Coronado**, written especially for students in the grade and high schools.

Coronado's return to Mexico was an unhappy and tiresome journey. Along the way, many of his men departed the main army to return to their homes. Therefore when Coronado reached Mexico City his army had shrunk to possibly one hundred men.

Although the Viceroy could not be happy with the Coronado report, he did not blame Don Francisco. He had obviously done his best. The recital of his search for treasure, the suffering, hunger and diseases which had been endured by the men, gave the report the tone of an unparalleled saga.

Returning to his office as Governor of New Galicia, in 1544, there was much criticism of Coronado to follow. Some thought he had been neglectful of his duties as Governor, some claimed he had given high posts in his army not on merit, but to men who were his friends. Others insisted he had treated the natives with unnecessary cruelty and had allowed them to be used as slaves. All this agitation resulted in Coronado being brought to trial. He was convicted on some of the charges. Significantly he was ordered by the Judge to relinquish his office as Governor, and to pay a substantial fine.

Coronado thereupon removed himself and family to Mexico City where, as a member of the town council, he remained until his death in 1554. Unknown to him, he had discovered for Spain what was eventually an immense portion of the richest country in the world, the United States of America.

The remains of Don Francisco, his celebrated wife Doña Beatriz, and other members of the explorer's family lie buried in the famous Church of Santo Domingo, in Mexico City. In the long view of history, he was indeed a conqueror!

Chapter 8
THE FRANCISCAN MISSIONS

Explorers, conquistadors, fortune hunters and the omnipresent Church had now established a European concept of civilization in the New World. The savagery of the Mexicans had been abated, and the natives had seen the cross substituted for the sword. The motivation of these seemingly unrelated series of events and accomplishments now becomes apparent. The recital of even so brief a history, the highlights, reveals with positive emphasis the truth that God has moved to bring Christ to this new continent. With all its complexity, the means remained a simple extension of Christ's injunction that his disciples take the Gospels to the whole world.

If these strange mutations needed a sign or proof of their profound objectives, no better example could be cited than the aggressive attitude of the Church following the failure of Coronado and his expedition. If the potential conqueror had abandoned this mighty but desolate territory, the Church seized upon it as an immense opportunity. The Franciscan missions are living proof of their indomitable spirit. The Spanish were colonizers as well as explorers, and other expeditions were to follow the great Coronado.

In 1598, Don Juan de Oñate came to the new land and established the first colony to be settled in the American Southwest by Europeans. To give this event its proper perspective, this New Mexican settlement was made nine years before Jamestown was founded by the English; ten years before Quebec was founded by the great French explorer Champlain; and it was twenty-two years later that the pilgrims landed at Plymouth Rock!

The most striking difference between the attitude of the Spanish versus the English who arrived on the Atlantic coast was the approach to the complex Indian problem. While the Protestants from Europe treated the Indians as a conquered people, the Spanish

men of God regarded them as human beings and approached them with the cross. History is either confused, or these facts have been deliberately concealed, for early American history was written obviously with a New England accent.

The humane treatment of the Indian, regardless of revolts and many hesitations, has resulted in an Indian attitude which grows with each year. Overwhelmingly the Indians of New Mexico who have been converted are Catholics, due to the understanding of the priest. They did not frown on native rites when these Indian ceremonies did not conflict with Christian principles.

Originally a few Franciscan priests trudged across the blistering, discouraging deserts. Water holes were days apart, the Indians often hostile and there was little resembling food. These courageous padres founded a mission on the Rio Grande River at old Puaray pueblo, now in Sandoval county, New Mexico. This was the beginning, and for two hundred years the building of mission edifices never ceased. During that period forty-nine missions, not to mention visitas (branch missions without resident padres) were constructed; it is significant that six-

teen still are used for worship after nearly
four hundred years. Approximately twenty-
five stand in ruins and no trace is left of many
of the Arizona missions. Only San Xavier del
Bac is restored and very actively in use.

During the period between 1598 and 1608
a total of more than eight thousand Indians
were converted to Catholicism by the old time
padres. And by 1617 it is estimated that there
were nearly fourteen thousand neophytes as
a result of the zeal of the Church. This is
without parallel in any other section of the
United States or by any other religious organization. Something to stir our imagination
and invoke our deepest admiration.

Each of the missions has its history, its
romance, its great deeds and its singular
accomplishments. We have selected two for
the purposes of this book as they are still in
use in the year 1960.

San Miguel Church (Saint Michael) was
erected by Don Juan de Oñate between 1605
and 1608, and is one of the oldest places of
worship in North America. It is the pride of
Santa Fe, the capital of New Mexico. San
Miguel is as old as Santa Fe itself as Oñate
began is construction immediately after
founding the city. It has had a tumultuous

history, and for long periods of time, stood in ruins. Built to save souls, it has known bloody conflict including the Pueblo revolt in 1680. It was a real center and outpost of Christianity when General Kearney with his Army of the West entered the city in 1846 and also when the Confederates captured Santa Fe in 1862. When built it was an important adjunct of the ancient Indian district called **The Analco** (the area given over exclusively to the friendly Tlaxcalan who accompanied Oñate to Santa Fe). It served the Indians as a mission church until the Spaniards were driven out in 1680. It is interesting to note that when the Indians in rebellion took over the town, only the roof of the church was destroyed.

Wind and sun worked their havoc until 1692 when General Diego de Vargas, came from Mexico and recaptured the city for the Spanish. The church was then repaired, but its full restoration was the work of Marquéz de la Peñuela in 1710, as proven by an ancient Spanish inscription on the main beam of the gallery; translated into English it reads, "The Marquéz de la Peñuela rebuilt this building; the Royal Ensign Don Augustín Flores Vergara, his servant, A.D. 1710."

The history this church could record! The military, the grandees and other notables would come to life. For as the western terminus of the celebrated Santa Fe trail the capital became the target of a vast western movement that amazingly extended the resources of a nation. In this city General Lew Wallace, then Governor of the Territory of New Mexico wrote many books including his fabulous **Ben Hur.** And the Governor often visited San Miguel church. Today, services are held regularly in the old but sturdy building. The altar and the reredos have again been restored and it is the very much used church of St. Michael's High School. Its history is far from complete.

San Xavier del Bac is nine miles south of Tucson on the Papago Indian reservation. Gleaming brilliantly in the Arizona sun, it is the one Arizona mission which appears today as it did in its years of greatest glory. Surely it is one of the most beautiful and authentic architectural monuments of the Spanish missions, one of the noble buildings of our country.

From the adobe huts and the grass wickiups, the domes and towers of San Xavier rise skyward and guide the traveller just as they

did the Jesuit and Franciscan Fathers in days gone by. Once surrounded by gardens, fruit trees and flowers, nature had many times taken over and the landscaping had returned to mesquite, sage and cacti. But the grounds are once again improved and the building is superb.

San Xavier was founded by Father Kino in the spring of 1700. From that time until the Jesuits were expelled from all Spanish possessions in 1767, this was not only the most imposing, but the most prosperous mission in the entire Southwest. The first resident priest was Padre Francisco Gonzales, but following the death of Father Kino in 1711 the mission was abandoned as no white man entered Arizona until the rehabilitation of San Xavier about 1732. Fray Felipe Segesser was then in charge, but Fathers came and went without interference until in 1751, the Pima Indians rebelled. They plundered the church. Again it was left to the caprice of desert wind, storms and sun.

In June 1768, the first Franciscan in the person of Fray Francisco Garcés took charge, and with his coming San Xavier entered a new era. But Padre Garcés became ill and was sent to Guevavi, and during this time the

mission was partially destroyed by the Apaches. Raids continued at irregular intervals until about 1772 when a population of nearly three hundred began to take a firm stand against marauders. In the meantime the mission continued to be restored, although most of the vestments and ornaments were stolen and never reinstalled.

The decisive decline of San Xavier began about 1810 and this degeneration was hastened when the Franciscans were ordered out of Mexico in 1824 following a sweeping change in the Government. For many years no priest came near the beautiful church which was left to the merciless Apaches and the desert elements. But reconstruction began in earnest when Padre Battaser Cavillo came in 1883. With him came Padre Narcisco Gutierres who completed the structure much as we see it today. Both padres preached the gospel of love and when death ended their careers, the Papagos buried them in the church which thereupon became a monument to their devotion and heroism.

The story of San Xavier often reads like a surrealist dream, and its history is contrasted with acts of violence, valor, and of hospitality. After the expulsion of the Fran-

ciscans, for instance the faithful Papago Indians hid the sacred articles of the altar and the furnishings. For more than a quarter of a century wandering bands of Mexican or American outlaws sought shelter from sandstorms or the burning heat in this beautiful Church. Due entirely to the devotion of the Papagos, the building was not totally destroyed, When in 1859 a padre came to them, the Papagos hastily returned the furnishings, and joyfully rang the mission bells which had been silent some twenty-five years.

In the original plan for San Xavier del Bac, two towers were included, but only one was completed at the time. The natives tell the story of the other tower. When it was approximately one-half completed a priest, working on the masonry, fell and was killed; work stopped immediately and was not continued for many years.

Under the direction of Bishop Granjon, the modern restorations of San Xavier began in 1906. The wall around the church and the landscaping were reconstructed. The interior was completely redone, and is an example without parallel of Spanish Colonial art in America. As a church it demonstrates faith and courage. It stands as a small scale replica

of the tenacity, the power to rise from the
ashes and the eternal core that is the soul of
the Roman Catholic faith. As the faith and
the history of the Church have their scars, so
San Xavier. The bullet-scarred doorway
remains to tell of the grim years through
which it withstood violence, neglect and decay,
to final triumph.

The Spanish conquest of America then
embraced two major interests; the consolida-
tion of the gains in Mexico, and the spiritual
cultivation of the vast domains to the north.

The concern of this narrative is with the
fortunes of the Spanish in the great Southwest and particularly with the Church, the
missions and the padres. The victories and
the defeats make an arresting story. Far from
the amenities of their European homes, deprived of even the necessities of life, tramping
in sandals or barefoot over the excruciating
terrain, victim of sandstorm, scorching sun,
hostile Indians, these men relate in their
anguish and bitter tasks, as well as in their
positive faith, to St. Peter and St. Paul and
to the other Apostles who suffered unto death
for their belief.

Tied by the umbilical cord of faith with
Spain the missions eventually declined as

Spain itself withdrew in defeat from its summit of world power. But the seeds thus planted were to grow again, watered and tended by a new group of men. First the Bishops from France, and eventually as the United States grew to significant stature, in natural evolution came the priests of America.

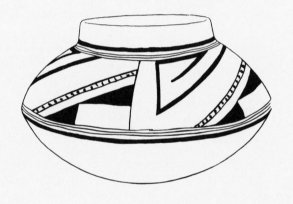

Chapter 9

SANTA FE:
THE ROYAL CITY
OF THE HOLY FAITH

The historian Bolton speaks of the Spanish
Jesuits and Franciscans as "a force which
made for the preservation of the Indians, as
opposed to their destruction, so characteristic
of the Anglo-American frontier."

But unfortunate changes had now come
about in the Southwest. The decline of Spain
as a world power logically had its effect on
the Church in America. When the Southwest
empire finally came to the United States under
the terms of the Mexican Treaty, Santa Fe,
the cradle of Catholicism in America could
no longer turn to the Bishop of Durango for
help in ecclesiastical affairs. The Church, the

74

faith and the people had indeed fallen on evil days. The once glorious series of missions and churches were actually falling apart in ruins. Spiritually, an even worse condition existed. Cut off from Spain, left to struggle alone, the mission schools were being abandoned. By 1850 there were but nine priests in this great territory. Ignorance had taken over, and even the Catholic Indians were left to their mixed memories of Christ, and were returning to the earth gods of their ancestors.

Meeting in Plenary Council in Baltimore in 1849, the American Bishops examined these apalling conditions. From this meeting came an answer that was to supply both a renaissance and a man of spiritual force to implement their actions. They immediately petitioned Pope Pius IX to establish New Mexico as a separate vicariate apostolic and remove it from the authority of Durango, Mexico. Most fortunate of all they nominated a young French missionary priest to be appointed administrator.

Bishop John Baptist Lamy was a striking figure, powerful, disciplined, but humane. When he was finally appointed and arrived in Santa Fe he received a tumultuous welcome from the people, but the clergy, never having

been officially informed of his appointment was cool and puzzled. Therefore, alone and on horseback, Bishop Lamy set out for the city of Durango, to clarify matters. Fifteen hundred strange and fearful miles. He returned with all his credentials, and henceforth Catholicism began the upward curve that brought it to the high plateau achieved by Archbishop Byrne, who has even succeeded in bringing the hostile Penitentes back to the fold.

With the advent of Bishop Lamy, the Church began to reassert its powers of recuperation which has characterized Roman Catholic institutions since St. Peter. The Bishop spent much of his time in the saddle. He brought encouragement and new life to parishes all over his enormous diocese, and exhibited the greatest fortitude in facing every sort of obstacle, from desert heat to the recalcitrant Indians. There are those who honestly believe that the transition from Spanish administration to that of the French Bishops could and would have been accomplished with less difficulty, pain and misunderstanding, had Lamy taken as next in command a Spanish man of God. But he elected another course and took the more difficult road. Cer-

tainly he was a romantic figure in the landscape of the American Southwest and his footprints will be visible to many future generations.

The story of Bishop Lamy is an American classic as told by Willa Cather in her **Death Comes for the Archbishop.** While this is fiction at its best, the qualities and the spirit of Lamy are true, and the book is based on one of the greatest men in the Catholic history of America.

Putting his diocese in order, Bishop Lamy almost immediately began the realization of his dream, a worthy Cathedral in the romantic and historic West. Collecting money not only from his flock, but from France and Mexico as well, he brought French architects and masons to ancient Santa Fe. Stones from the Arroyo Sais were used, as was the volcanic tufa from Cerro Mogino

It is perhaps unfortunate that Bishop Lamy did not build his temple in the New Mexican mission style. But at that time the city was destroying old adobe structures, and undoubtedly the kindly Bishop wished to introduce an element of European culture into the wild and wooly town of his headquarters.

Bishop Lamy cannot be mentioned without

introducing another great character who was to leave his imprint upon the West, the new Vicar General Father Joseph P. Macheboeuf, a fellow Frenchman, who later became Bishop of Denver. In 1875 the resourceful Lamy became the first Archbishop of Santa Fe. And in 1888, after an amazingly fruitful and saintly life, death came for the Archbishop.

He was succeeded by another French Bishop. John Baptist Salpointe had come from France in 1859. He first served as an assistant at the Cathedral, after which he was assigned to a parish. He was then sent to the Arizona area of the Santa Fe diocese where his exceptional work was recognized, and he became the first Vicar Apostolic of Arizona with headquarters at Tucson. His success there caused him to be transferred back to assist the old Archbishop of Santa Fe. In 1885 Salpointe became Archbishop of Santa Fe. Later, in retirement he wrote his **Soldiers of the Cross**, which earned him the title of historian of the kingdom.

Placid Louis Chapelle who became Archbishop of Santa Fe in 1895 came from France via St. Matthew's Church, Washington, D.C. During his short term as Archbishop, major

additions to the Cathedral were completed. His reception of the pallium was the occasion of ecclesiastical pomp heretofore unknown in the West. Among the ten prelates present was the very distinguished Cardinal Gibbons, the first Prince of the Church to visit the kingdom of St. Francis.

Following the transfer of Archbishop Chapelle to New Orleans, the saintly Bishop of Tucson, Peter Bourgade succeeded him. His bringing back of the Franciscans to Santa Fe, after sixty-six years of absence was his most notable achievement, and a matter of great historical significance. These were American friars, with headquarters in Cincinnati.

The last of the French prelates was Archbishop Pitaval, who succeeded Archbishop Bourgade in 1909. Under John Baptist Pitaval (the third John Baptist) many changes and betterments were made to the Cathedral, and in the diocese generally. On May 23rd, 1915, the bronze statue of Archbishop Lamy now in front of the Cathedral was dedicated, and on that occasion, Archbishop Pitaval and Governor MacDonald, the Governor of the new state of New Mexico, played leading parts.

The first American prelate, Archbishop Daeger, came in 1919. As Fray Angelico Chavez wrote, "He left no monument of note, no great pastoral letters; but he shed a heavenly impression on all he met as did a Little Poor Man in Italy over seven hundred years ago (St. Francis)."

Rudolph Aloysius Gerken followed Archbishop Daeger as the second American prelate to preside at the Cathedral. Not since the investiture with the pallium of Archbishop Chapelle in 1895 when the Cathedral itself was consecrated, had the venerable building welcomed so many Church dignitaries at one time.

Many changes took place under Archbishop Gerken. To commemorate both the fourth centenary of Coronado's entry in 1540 and the naming of the new kingdom of Saint Francis, the Archbishop caused the beautiful church of Cristo Rey to be built. Into this new church was then moved the great reredos from the Cathedral, a major operation. The reredos was taken down piecemeal and reassembled in the new church to grace its sanctuary. It is one of the most beautiful reredos in the entire West, if not in America. The prime cause of the removal was the faulty foundations of a portion of the Cathedral, since corrected. But

the reredos seems to be more harmonious and striking in the new church of Cristo Rey than it had been in the Cathedral, thus there is gain rather than loss in the removal.

The present Archbishop of Santa Fe, Edwin Vincent Byrne, came to the diocese in 1943 and has had an impact on New Mexico comparable to that of Archbishop Lamy. He has served God and his church all over the world. Born in Philadelphia, he was sent to such far flung missionary posts as the Philippines and Puerto Rico. There he served in the centuries-old diocese of San Juan. He is Santa Fe's eighth Archbishop, and one of the most active of the distinguished group. His outstanding achievements include the building of schools, hospitals, convents, seminaries, and other permanent installatians, and the reaffiliation with the Church of the Penitentes.

It is difficult for modern minds to believe that until very recently, when Archbishop Byrne succeeded in his difficult task, the grim realities of Penitente rites still existed. The stories about them seemed a myth from the dark ages, but the facts were gruesome and cruel. In the Penitente country of northern New Mexico, the traveller comes upon crosses, some on the summit of a hill, some in rocky

gorges, others seemingly hidden by cacti or sagebrush. Once they bore inscriptions, but the summer sun and winter snows have eroded these slender emblems of Christ. Each tell a silent story of self-inflicted torture, the like of which man has seldom witnessed.

Few have ever seen the cruifixion with its Cristo, cross bearers and whipping brothers. These beat their own naked backs with cacti or iron whips until, not infrequently, their very life-blood was scattered over the desert sands along the line of march. Onlookers were resented, and on occasion, so rumor goes, disappeared mysteriously. The Penitente brothers or Brothers of Light, were found in Sandoval, San Miguel, Mora, Taos, Colfax, Rio Arriba and Valencia counties. Each community had a meeting house or morada, built of stone or more often of adobe. Travellers know when they are in Penitente country by the moradas and the crosses which often make arresting symbols outlined against the setting sun. Although the ceremonies took place several times a year, the most important occured during the Lenten season, reaching a climax on Good Friday.

But they are now back into the fold, after years of darkness and ignorance. When final

repentence came, they journeyed in a body to Santa Fe, where Archbishop Byrne met and blessed them on the steps of the Cathedral. In this moving scene, the Penitentes bowed down and kissed the foot of His Excellency, thus signifying their complete subjugation to Christ, and their future loyalty to the true rites of the Catholic Church.

The old Cathedral in Santa Fe is wrapped in a cocoon of tradition and stirring events, both secular and religious. One feels these emanations when passing through its doors into the interior. Some of the greatest churchmen of the Catholic faith have given it an aura, as have the numberless devout parishioners and visitors who have entered its portals. And in addition to its ancient history its walls have witnessed some remarkably modern events. As an example, His Excellency Archbishop Byrne welcomed the suggestion that Igor Stravinsky conduct his **Threni**: The Lamentations of Jeremiah, in the Cathedral. This extraordinary concert took place on July 12, 1959. The Cathedral was packed, and hundreds heard the new work outside the structure via loud speakers. It was the only time that an American Cathedral had been the scene of such a program. The

precedent went back a year or more, when the present Pope John XXIII had welcomed Stravinsky in the Cathedral of Venice, Italy, where he conducted a new work. The Pope then Cardinal Roncalli, was Patriarch of Venice.

The once western terminus of the famous Santa Fe trail, the diminutive city has preserved its own special character and atmosphere. One readily accepts the fact that this is the oldest Capital city in the United States. For many reasons it is a place of national importance. It gave its name, for instance, to our largest railway system, **The Atchison, Topeka and Santa Fe.** Its many museums of art, archeology, ancient Spanish exhibits as well as the artifacts of the Indian attract cosmopolitan visitors. Here Fred Harvey has long estabished one of his most unique and hospitable hotels, **La Fonda**, with its many colored furniture, Mexican tin-framed mirrors and piñon beamed ceilings. In addition to all these and other attractions that have made it the tourist center of the Southwest, its distinguished summer opera festival, and its annual Fiesta draw people from all over the world. Santa Fe is not easily forgotten.

EPILOGUE

With the Church healthy and firmly established all over the Southwest, indeed, all over America, the recruitment of the Penitentes seems to place a period at the end of this book. Christ has, through a most improbable and curious route, come to the New World in a measure never guessed by the hardy band who believed in Him in the beginning.

The stories of heroism, or remarkable occurences too fantastic to be accidental, crowd for acceptance as this book came to a close. There is Padre Eusebio Francisco Kino, a man who seems to defy the inventions of fiction, and who holds the same positon in the Sonora and southern Arizona mission field as Padre Junipero Serra has in California. Both were inspired and saintly men. There is the incredible but insistant story of the native American Indians who told Coronado and his men that they had met a Christian before, whom they called the **Lady in Blue,** and of the American

85

Archbishop who, a few years ago, went out of his way to find a little convent in Spain where the nuns wore blue habits. There, to his astonishment, he found documents that attested to the fact that one of their ancestors had indeed visited the Indians centuries before, in America.

There is the magnificent record of Fray Francisco Atanasio Dominguez. In 1775 he was sent to New Mexico from the Mexican Province of the Holy Gospel, with orders to make a complete detailed report on both the spiritual and economic status of the New Mexican missions. By this method he would serve "both Majesties" as he put it, for such a report would be useful to the royal authorities in formulating their frontier policy, and to the Franciscans in promoting the spiritual welfare of the vast and little known region.

Father Dominguez, travelling on foot, visited every mission in the territory. Either he had a great sense of humor, or he was the most observant, methodical and conscientious man that ever lived. For the good Father reported everything. First he made drawings of the mission or the Church. Then he stated the spiritual and moral atmosphere of the Padre and the Church, invoiced the furnish-

ings, described and reported every cranny of the Padre's mind. This constitutes a document unique in this world. So honest was he, that soon he found himself attacked by those who had the most to suffer, or the most to lose from the truth as Father Dominguez so zealously reported it. After all this agonizing work, travail and unendurable conditions of living, Father's report, written in longhand on parchment was filed away in the archives of Mexico City with a sarcastic notation and forgotten. It was discovered there in 1928, a historical mine of information about life and society in eighteenth-century New Mexico. The meticulous record of the most commonplace appurtenances of every day life makes this document uniquely valuable.

We owe the discovery of this document to the patience, learning, and discernment of Dr. France Vinton Scholes, outstanding historian of colonial Hispanic America. In 1956, the full Dominguez report, translated by Eleanor B. Adams and Fray Angelico Chavez, was published in a handsome book designed by Roland F. Dickey by the University of New Mexico Press. It became another exhibit in the monumental pile of evidence that they were spiritual giants who brought Christ to

America and kept His spirit alive through every vicissitude.

The acts of heroism, the incidents without number which finally got into the pages of history, not to mention the countless martyrdoms that are unknown except to God, are woven into the rich fabric of the Southwest. Dear Padre Francisco Tomás Garcés, for instance, the little man with the big cross; or Father Martinez of Taos fame; each deserve a book to themselves.

But one of the most extraordinary exploits favored by this writer is what happened to the final phases of the de Miera expedition. The Governor of New Mexico had urged de Miera to organize a group of men with the possibility of finding a route to the newly established Monterey in California; or at least colonize the vast area which comprises what is now a large part of New Mexico, Arizona and Colorado, and all of what is now Utah and Nevada. This was a large order, indeed. No white man had ever trod foot on this vast country and returned. But de Miera believed that if he continued westwardly far enough, he would sooner or later come to the Pacific ocean, a very fair assumption. It was the inability to traverse this country, mostly

desert, that offered the problem. For water and food were unknown and proved to be non-existent.

The party set forth on July 29, 1776. Under de Miera, the next important man was a Spanish priest, Padre Francisco Atanasio Dominguez, previously mentioned in this epilogue. Third in command was another remarkable man, a Spanish padre, Silvestre Velez de Escalante. The two Fathers had only a minor interest in the main purpose of this trip, which was the extension of trade; they were mightily interested in taking the faith to the Indians who **must** be in the wilderness. If there was a country that did not know the cross, the only answer was, **onward!**

Nothing was heard from the party in Santa Fe, their starting point, for over six months. In 1777, sometime in January, the party arrived back in Santa Fe, and as far as the objectives were concerned, the whole expedition had been a failure. They found no new trade routes, they seemingly had made no converts, they had found few natives to exploit. Therefore, Santa Fe wanted to know what they had been occupied with all that time, and the only answer forthcoming was that they had been walking. Walking was the

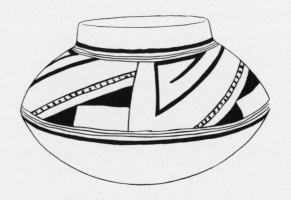

correct answer, for they had covered more than sixteen hundred miles by direct route, and if you counted side trips, they had actually walked over two thousand miles.

The backers of the expedition had lost their money, the whole thing was an unmitigated fiasco. But there are overtones that can only now be seen. Had the party continued and had not been forced back by thirst, hunger and hostile natives, they would have eventually ventured further to the north, and clashed with United States forces. There might have been a very different chapter written in what is called the "Mexican War."

The most curious element of this whole disappointing affair was the manner in which the name Escalante, from the day the illfated group returned, had continued to rise in importance. De Miera was the leader, and in the records, Dominguez' name always follows that of the leader. Escalante is always third. It is a euphonious name, possibly more appealing to the Anglo-Saxon ear than the name of either of the other men. But that alone could not account for the fact that Escalante is today such a figure.

In 1869 nearly a hundred years after the de Miera expedition failed, semi-illiterate men

were familiar with the name Escalante. This was the year that Major Powell and his boatmen battled their way down the omnivorous teeming Colorado River. One of his boatmen refers to the great padre in a letter he wrote home, spelling his name phonetically as "Esklanty." From the ten men who made this historic trip with de Miera, posterity had selected Escalante as the one name to survive among students of the American West. There are many who to this day take it for granted that this was Escalante's expedition, that he was the leader and the important man. What almost two hundred years can do to history! For anyone who wants to know of this expedition in detail the diary kept by Escalante is available, but we are here concerned with the most remarkable and unexplained incident of what must have been a soul-searching and body-damaging expedition.

Leaving Santa Fe with pack animals and horses, the party had moved northward, reaching their furthest point on September 13, 1776. This was not too far from what is now the city of Provo, Utah. Nothing here resembled a route to California, and the most forbidding of the deserts which the party faced is to this day called the Escalante desert.

Things were coming to a crisis. The trip was away off schedule, the food was low, the hardship acute.

In October they were in the neighborhood of the present Utah-Arizona border, and snow was falling in the high mountains. Apparently, in this emergency, the nearest point for relief was Santa Fe itself, and a council was called to make a decision. Taking the whole desperate situation into account, a vote was cast and the two padres very sensibly voted to return. Anything else was madness and death. But the contingent that wanted to proceed on to California was not satisfied, and the resourceful Escalante suggested that they let the decision rest with God. Lots were drawn; a short stick, Santa Fe; a long stick, California! As Dominguez provided the prayers, Escalante provided the sticks, and the leader de Miera was given the honor of drawing first. We can see him hesitate, look east, look west, and then draw with eyes closed. He drew the short stick, and it was Santa Fe.

By one of those psychological but unstated progressions of power, at that moment the leadership passed from the hands of the explorer to the Church. Dominguez and Escal-

ante took over. But the problem of the return was by no means resolved. They were in deserts, badlands and mountains. But a change of leadership had raised the spirits of the party, and the two priests, after carefully taking their bearings, set out for Santa Fe.

It is obvious that had not Escalante and God contrived to halt this mad adventure, all would have soon perished either in the snow and ice of the mountains, or the waterless deserts. Anyone who has ever experienced the blistering Nevada landscape will say amen to that.

Taking a shorter route than they had traversed outward bound, the party was led by Escalante and Dominguez southward into Arizona. Completely unknown to them but exactly in their path, lay the colossal, impossible gorge of the Grand Canyon. But when they had unknowingly proceeded to within a few miles of this great barrier and were still in the Kaibab forest, faith took over. The padres turned east, missed the rim of the Grand Canyon, and threaded along what is now the Arizona-Utah border. Although they could not actually have known how close they were to the Grand Canyon, or that it was

there at all, they must have sensed the danger, and carefully avoided it.

Eastward they wearily trudged, through the Kaibab Plateau. Unknown to them, they walked in an almost scientificaly straight line towards the one chance they had for survival, a point where the Colorado River **could** be crossed. It was life or death and every hour counted. But the padres led their party with supreme confidence to the river's bank. Possibly this particular manifestation of divine guidance is so exciting to the writer because he has been over this territory on foot, on horseback, by motorcar and aeroplane. From the eastern end of the Grand Canyon itself, to miles above Glen Canyon the Colorado River runs in a channel from a thousand to twelve hundred feet deep, mostly of red sanstone. It is perpendicular; might have been cut by a gigantic cheese-knife; I would have sworn that no human being, or no machine other than an aeroplane could cross the river for several hundred miles though this particular part of the Colorado River system.

Yet the padres and their party came to the bank of the river at a point almost directly east of Kanab, Utah. Here, unknown and unseen, was a slight canyon, so steep that when

they led their horses down it, footholds had to be dug to support the animals' hoofs. Furthermore, at this place, the river usually boils with currents and vortex.

Had the Escalante party arrived at the river a hundred yards upstream, or a hundred yards downstream from the spot at which they **did** arrive, they never could have seen, nor been aware that a possible exit down the river existed. I have experienced this erie sensation and marvelled at the miracle. But the padres arrived. Calmly they surveyed the scene, judged the odds, arranged the tactics, got their horses and mules finally down to the river and swam them across!

They had reached the river on November 7, 1776. The priests were not worried, but anyone else would have been. The river is usually high at this point, quicksand is treacherous, and crossing in high water is certain death. Therefore, high water would have meant death either by drowning, or starvation had they elected not to cross. But the water was low, and cross it they did.

A certified copy of the diary kept by Escalante was made by one of the Southwest's best historians, Charles F. Lummis. A rough translation reads:

... here the river is very wide and judging by the course it runs not very deep; but only by means of an adjacent canyon would one be able to descend to it. We sent two of our men to examine the canyon as well as the ford of the river, and they came back saying it would be too difficult. We did not give much credence to this information and we ourselves, accompanied by Don Juan Pedro Cisneros are determined to examine it tomorrow ... Seventh day. We went early to inspect the canyon and ford and taking the two Muniz brothers as they might be able to cross the river, they being good swimmers. In descending the said canyon it was necessary for the protection of the animals to make steps with an axe in a large rock for a distance of three rods or little less. By this means the horses were able to pass, although without goods or packs. We went down the canyon, walked one mile and arrived at the river; and we continued along the narrow strip of shore near the water to its very limit which brought us to the widest part of the stream. And here, it appeared, was a ford.

This then is a literal picture of the crossing of the Colorado by the first white men to make the attempt. As are so many heroic statements by men of God, it is masterpiece of understatement. The last lap of the trip into Oraibi, the mesa pueblo of the Hopi Indians offered hospitality, water, and food.

If chances of a thousand to one are a miracle, then this is indubitably a miracle of faith. For two stalwart, pious, optimistic padres, whose trust never faltered, aided by a couple of sticks, one short and one long, had won.

Escalante is a name that will forever loom in American history of the West. Already the exploit of the two padres has received the supreme modern accolade. On the maps which the oil companies furnish motorists can be seen, just above the Arizona border on the Colorado River and in red letters, the words, "The Crossing of the Fathers."

Manzanita Ranch

February 1960

BIBLIOGRAPHY

(In the order in which the material was read by the outhor.)

The Discovery and Conquest of Mexico by Bernal Diaz del Castillo (Farrar, Straus and Cudahy)

Admiral of the Ocean Sea by Samuel Eliot Morison (Little, Brown)

Coronado's Seven Cities by George P. Hammond

Coronado, Knight of Pueblos and Plains by Herbert E. Bolton (Whittlesly House)

Odyssey of Cabeza de Vaca by Morris Bishop (Century Company)

The Journey of Fray Marcos de Niza by Clive Hollenbeck (University Press in Dallas)

Zumarraga and the Mexican Inquisition by Richard E. Greenleaf (Manuscript)

The Gardens of Flower, Wing, Song and Star by Aileen O'Bryan (Manuscript)

Listen, Bright Angel by Edwin Corle (Duell, Sloan and Pearce)

Publications of the Historical Society of New Mexico

The Spanish Pioneers, etc. by Charles F. Lumis (A. C. McClurg & Co.)

Missions and Pueblos of the old Southwest by Earle R. Forrest (Arthur H. Clark Company)

American Catholicism by John Tracy Ellis (University of Chicago Press)

Commerce of the Prairies by Josiah Gregg (University of Oklahoma Press)

Rim of Christendom by Herbert Eugene Bolton (Macmillan Company)

The Benavides Memorial by Messrs. Hodge, Hammond and Rey (University of New Mexico Press)

Religious Architecture of New Mexico by George Kubler
(Taylor Museum)

History of Hawikuh by Frederick Webb Hodge

Mission Monuments of New Mexico by Hewett and Fisher
(University of New Mexico Press)

Landmarks of New Mexico by Hewett and Mauzy (University
of New Mexico Press)

Acoma, the Sky City by Mrs. Williams T. Sedgwick (Harvard
University Press)

Spanish Mission Churches of New Mexico by Bradford Prince
(Torch Press)

Spanish Exploration in the Southwest by H. E. Bolton
(Charles Scribner Sons)

The Centuries of Santa Fe by Paul Horgan (E. P. Dutton)

Diego de Vargas by Jessie B. Bailey (University of New
Mexico Press)

New Mexico by Erna Fergusson (Alfred A. Knopf)

Sky Determines by Ross Calvin (University of New Mexico
Press)

La Conquistadora by Fray Angelico Chavez (St. Anthony
Guild Press)

Archives of the Archdiocese of Santa Fe (Academy of
American Franciscan History)

New Mexican Village Arts by Roland F. Dickey (University
of New Mexico Press)

The Colorado by Frank Waters (Rhinehart & Company)

Desert Country by Edwin Corle (Duell, Sloan and Pearce)

Brothers of Light by Alice Corbin Henderson (Harcourt,
Brace & Company)

Aztecs of Mexico by George C. Vaillant (Doubleday, Doran)

The Ancient Maya by Sylvanus G. Morley (Stanford University
Press)

ACKNOWLEDGMENT

My first indebtedness is to Peter Ribera Ortega whose family has resided in Santa Fe since its founding. His research and counsel have been invaluable and decisive as he is a scholar deeply interested in the subject matter of this book.

His Excellency, The Most Reverend Edwin V. Byrne, Archbishop of Santa Fe gave much encouragement to this work, as did two members of his staff the Reverend Francis Tournier and the Reverend O. A. Coggiola-Mower.

Lawrence Clark Powell made available the extraordinary Spanish and Southwest volumes of the University of California in Los Angeles. His assistant, Gordon Williams was extremely helpful.

Mary Coleman Powell lent rare volumes from her personal library.

Isabelle Armitage edited this work and typed the final manuscript.

1500 copies of this book have been designed by Merle Armitage and printed by
Lynton R. Kistler for the Academy
Library Guild. Set in Intertype Ideal type,
and printed on Sunray Vellum paper.
Bound by Weber-McCrea. The four drawings on the insert are by Edward O'Brien.
End sheet drawings by Merle Armitage
and P. G. Napolitano. Aztec, Mayan, Hopi,
Zuni and Navajo forms and figures are
from the publications of the Laboratory
of Anthropology, Santa Fe.

1964

Date Due

DEM 94